SEASON SWAP

Carmel Reilly

OXFORD
UNIVERSITY PRESS

OXFORD
UNIVERSITY PRESS

Great Clarendon Street, Oxford, OX2 6DP, United Kingdom

Oxford University Press is a department of the University
of Oxford. It furthers the University's objective of excellence
in research, scholarship, and education by publishing
worldwide. Oxford is a registered trade mark of Oxford
University Press in the UK and in certain other countries

Text © Carmel Reilly 2014

British Library Cataloguing in Publication Data
Data available

ISBN: 978-0-19-830805-8

10 9 8 7 6 5 4 3 2 1

Paper used in the production of this book is a natural,
recyclable product made from wood grown in sustainable
forests. The manufacturing process conforms to the
environmental regulations of the country of origin.

Printed in China by Hing Yip

Acknowledgements

Series Editor: Nikki Gamble

Designed and typeset by Fiona Lee, Pounce Creative

Photography by Lindsay Edwards
Illustrations by Natalie Hughes

Cover photographs by Lindsay Edwards;
cover illustration by Fiona Lee

The publishers would like to thank the following for the permission
to reproduce photographs: **p8b:** Mint Images - Frans Lanting/Getty
Images; **p8tr:** Josef Friedhuber/Getty Images; **p9t:** ChinaPhotoPress/
Getty Images; **p12br:** Frans Lanting/Corbis; **p13b:** Konrad Wothe/
Minden Pictures/Corbis; **p13t:** Luong Thai Linh/Corbis/epa;
p16r: Hemis/Alamy; **p16tc:** Tom Reichner/Shutterstock;
p16tl: Donald M. Jones/Minden Pictures/Corbis; **p17t:** AFP/Getty
Images; **p20tl:** Jason Persoff Stormdoctor/Getty Images/Cultura
Science; **p21b:** DEA Picture Library/UIG/Rex Features;
p21t: Smileus/Shutterstock

Contents

Opposite Sides of the World   4

Summer/Winter   6

Autumn/Spring   10

Winter/Summer   14

Spring/Autumn   18

Season Swap!   22

Glossary and Index   24

To read this book, sometimes you'll need to turn it upside down!

Opposite Sides of the World

I'm Jack and I live in Manchester in the United Kingdom (UK). I'm going to tell you about the seasons in my part of the world – the **northern hemisphere**.

I'm Annabel and I live in Melbourne in Australia, which is in the **southern hemisphere**.

Did you know that while it's summer in the UK, it's winter in Australia? That's because the UK and Australia are on opposite sides of the world!

Seasons and the Sun

Earth moves around the Sun. It takes one year for it to go all the way around.

This picture shows lots of sunlight shining on the northern hemisphere. This means it is summer. Less sunlight is shining on the southern hemisphere. This means it is winter.

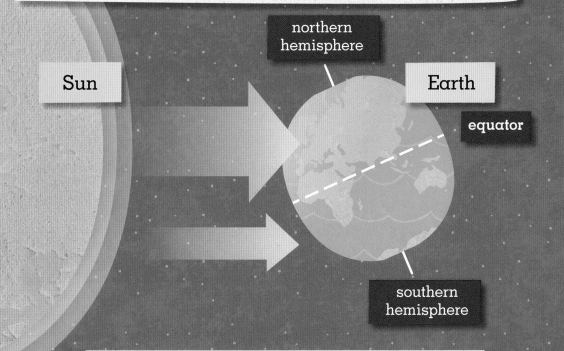

northern hemisphere

Sun

Earth

equator

southern hemisphere

When Earth moves around to the other side of the Sun, the seasons change. It is winter in the northern hemisphere and summer in the southern hemisphere.

Summer

Summer means swimming, bike rides and cricket.

Summer days can be warm and they are also long. The sun is still up when I go to bed!

Temperature for Melbourne

Temperature (degrees Celsius)

Aug | July | June

0
5
10
15
20
25
30

On the longest night of winter in Melbourne, there are 14 hours of darkness.

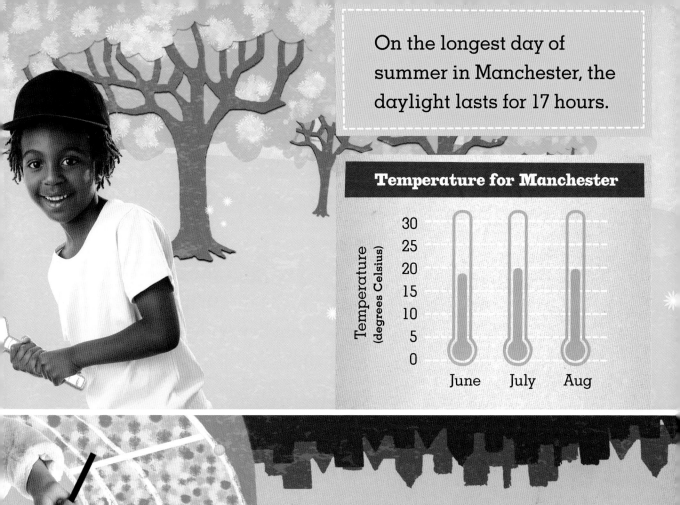

On the longest day of summer in Manchester, the daylight lasts for 17 hours.

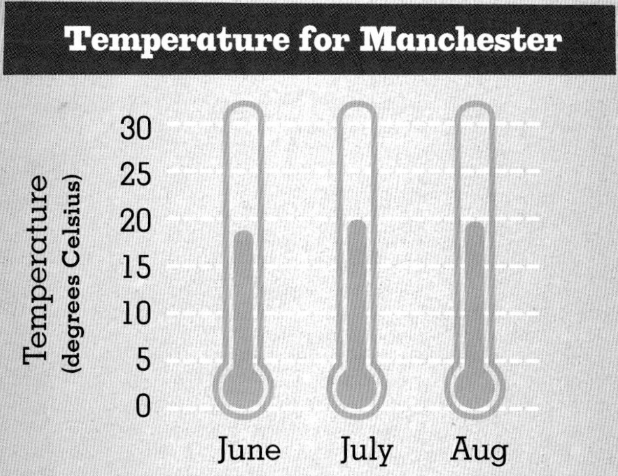
Temperature for Manchester
Temperature (degrees Celsius)
30
25
20
15
10
5
0
June
July
Aug

Winter

On winter weekends, I play netball and watch football.
It doesn't snow in Melbourne but we can drive to the mountains to ski.

It's **SUMMER** in the northern hemisphere.

Polar bears live in the Arctic. They can live without food in summer!

Emperor penguins are the only animals in Antarctica that have their babies during winter.

Manchester, UK
(Jack lives here!)

Heavy rain falls in East Asia in summer.

Melbourne, Australia
(Annabel lives here!)

It's **WINTER** in the southern hemisphere.

Autumn

In autumn, it gets dark in the early evening.

There is morning fog and lots of rain – and there are crunchy autumn leaves everywhere!

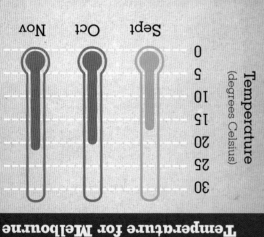

Temperature for Melbourne

Sept	Oct	Nov

Temperature (degrees Celsius)

0
5
10
15
20
25
30

SCHOOL

In September, the daytime temperature in Manchester and the night-time temperature in Melbourne are almost the same.

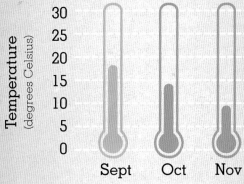

Temperature for Manchester

Temperature (degrees Celsius)

30
25
20
15
10
5
0

Sept   Oct   Nov

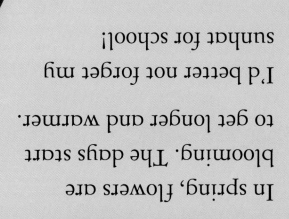

Spring

In spring, flowers are blooming. The days start to get longer and warmer. I'd better not forget my sunhat for school!

It's **AUTUMN** in the northern hemisphere.

It's **SPRING** in the southern hemisphere.

When spring arrives in South Africa, wild flowers burst into bloom.

Tet Trung Thu in Vietnam is a huge festival held in the middle of autumn.

In New Zealand, Little Penguins lay their eggs in spring.

Winter

When it snows, I love sledging, having snowball fights and building snowmen.

I warm up again indoors by helping Mum make food for our Christmas party.

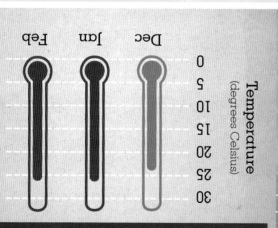

Temperature for Melbourne

Temperature (degrees Celsius)

Dec	Jan	Feb

0, 5, 10, 15, 20, 25, 30

The days are long in Melbourne during summer. Sometimes it doesn't get dark until nine o'clock.

The days get shorter during winter in Manchester. People go home from work and school in the dark!

Temperature for Manchester

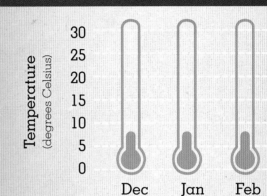

Temperature (degrees Celsius): 30, 25, 20, 15, 10, 5, 0

Dec   Jan   Feb

NEW YEAR'S EVE FIREWORKS!

Summer

Hooray for summer holidays! On New Year's Eve, there's a huge party in the city with fireworks and music. Tomorrow, we're going to the beach for some fun in the sun.

The North American snowshoe hare is usually brown but it turns white in winter.

It's **WINTER** in the northern hemisphere.

It's **SUMMER** in the southern hemisphere.

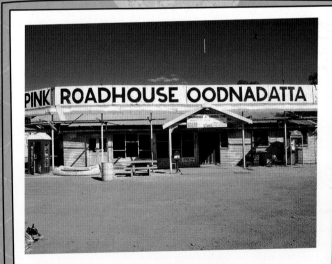

In Oodnadatta, South Australia, on 2nd January 1960, it was 50.7 degrees Celsius!

Sadeh is a festival of fire held in the Middle East in winter.

Spring

Some days in spring are warm and sunny, and others are cold and rainy. I like the rain!

We see lots of baby animals at the city farm near our house. There are baby sheep and horses!

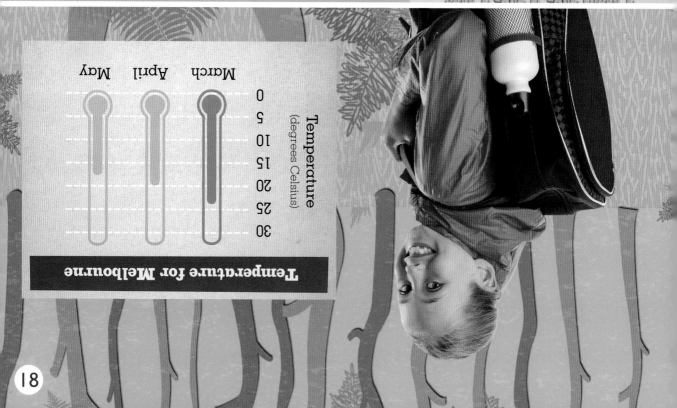

Temperature for Melbourne

Temperature (degrees Celsius)

March	April	May

0
5
10
15
20
25
30

Around 22nd March in Manchester and Melbourne, daytime and night-time are both about 12 hours long.

Temperature for Manchester

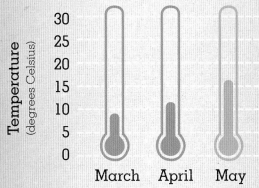

Temperature (degrees Celsius)

	March	April	May

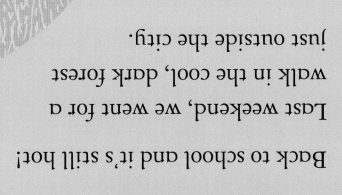

Autumn

Back to school and it's still hot!

Last weekend, we went for a walk in the cool, dark forest just outside the city.

It's **SPRING** in the northern hemisphere.

Tornado Alley is a part of the United States of America where there are a lot of tornadoes in spring.

It's **AUTUMN** in the southern hemisphere.

Cherry blossoms are the first sign of spring in Japan.

On Easter Island, the wettest time of year is late autumn.

Season Swap!

Our families are going to swap houses next year.

I can't wait to find out what the weather is like on the other side of the world. Will it really be hot in December?

I'm going to spend a whole year in Manchester. Jack said he'd leave me his sledge in case it snows.

I'm going to leave my bodyboard so Jack can ride the waves at the beach.

The distance between Manchester and Melbourne is almost 17000 kilometres!

Manchester, UK

Melbourne, Australia

The trip takes about 24 hours on an aeroplane!

Glossary

degrees Celsius: a measure of how hot or cold something is

equator: an imaginary line around the centre of the Earth, at the point where the Earth is widest

northern hemisphere: the half of the planet that is north of the equator

southern hemisphere: the half of the planet that is south of the equator

Index

Australia	4, 9, 16, 23
autumn	10, 12–13, 19, 20–21
dark	10, 14, 15, 19
daylight	7
fog	10
leaves	10
Manchester	4, 7, 9, 11, 15, 19, 22, 23
Melbourne	4, 6, 7, 9, 10, 11, 14, 18, 19, 23
rain	9, 10, 18
snow	7, 14, 22
spring	11, 12–13, 18, 20–21
summer	4, 5, 6–7, 8–9, 14–15, 16
sun	5, 6, 15
temperature	6, 7, 10, 11, 14, 15, 18, 19
United Kingdom (UK)	4, 9, 23
winter	4, 5, 6–7, 8–9 14–15, 16–17